Linda Parsons 2025

The author asserts the moral right under the Copyright, Designs and Patents Act 1988 to be identified as the author of this work. All Rights reserved. No part of this publication may be reproduced, stored in a retrieval system or transmitted, in any form or by any means without the prior consent of the author, nor be otherwise circulated in any form of binding or cover other than that which it is published and without a similar condition being imposed on the subsequent purchaser.

Contents

Am I too proud

Bromsgrove

Lean on God

My friend

Remember

Ode to the mice

You ask me

As together we've come

As years pass by

Tis Christmas time

As you walk along life's way

Hallalujah

Psalm 23

Holy Spirit

Shades of time

Amidst the turmoil and strife

Let us join together as one

Come my children

Jesus is here

Am I too proud

Am I too proud

To offer my hand

When another person

Needs help along the way?

Do I think of myself

As more worthy

Than to help

The poor man on the street?

Am I too afraid

Of what others may think

If I make it clear

That I know the Lord?

Do I want to go away

And hide, rather than

Show others that

God is on my side?

What should I do?

Be bold, be strong,

Let others know

That in my heart there

Is a song.

Stand tall and declare

That Jesus is lord.

Join the angels and sing,

ALLELIEU JESUS IS KING.

BROMSGROVE

There upon a hill;

It's steeple high above the town,

A church stands

Looking down

On the people passing by,

From it's walls

Comes a cry:-

OH LITTLE TOWN IN WORCESTERSHIRE
DID YOU KNOW THAT JESUS IS LIVING HERE?

The wind rustles

Through the trees around

Whose leaves fall upon the ground,

A small voice

Whispers in the grass

To the people as they pass:-

OH LITTLE IN WORCESTERSHIRE
DID YOU KNOW THAT JESUS IS LIVING HERE?

Lean on God

In this time of unrest

Lean on God

For He knows best.

When the going gets tough

Lean on God

Don't give up.

When things don't go your way

Lean on God

He won't let you go astray.

When you feel down and in despair

Lean on God

You're in His care.

When You're shocked and dismayed

Lean on God

Remember, the price He paid.

When you've lost the way,

Lean on God

His will, just trust and obey.

My Friend

As the clouds drift across the sky,

Many days in life pass by.

Sometimes things and places we forget,

Even people we've met.

Then along comes one

With whom you share,

The things in life

For which you care.

Margaret was one

Who my life did touch.

We laughed, we cried,

We raised our voices in song

We often sighed.

Together, on a Monday

We'd hit Dartford town,

Believe you me

In the shops we'd let our hair down.

Now as the time has come

To say goodbye

I can hear you

Singing with the angels on high.

We, your family and friends on earth,

Say thankyou for all the precious memories

We hold dear in each heart

To remember, As for a while we part.

REMEMBER

Remember,

When you are afraid,

Lost and alone,

Do not be anxious;

Remember,

When you have to climb

a mountain high,

You become tired and worn;

Remember,

When your limbs ache

and you're in pain,

Uncomfortable and sore;

Remember,

When you've finally

reached your goal,

Remember,

The keeper of your soul.

Remember,

Whatever in life may befall,

Remember Me,

Jesus,

The Lord of all.

Ode to the Mice

Dear Mr. and Mrs Mouse,

Please,please

This is our house.

We wish to

Eat and sleep

In peace;

So all running

Through our house

Must cease.

So if

A room for you,

May be free,

This we're afraid

Just cannot be.

So on this

And every day,

Please get the message,

AND JUST KEEP AWAY!

Written a few years ago for Tim and Caroline, who were having problems with mice in their

home at the time.

You ask me

You ask me

Who is Jesus?

JESUS IS MY SAVIOUR AND FRIEND,

One on whom

I can depend.

He is the one

who gave his all

For men who

From grace did fall.

He is the one,

Who day by day

Listens to me when I pray.

He is the one

Who entered this earth,

With a simple stable birth.

You ask me

Who is Jesus?

He is the reason

That I live,

Is always ready to forgive

When I fall along the way,

In his loving arms forever I'll stay.

You ask me

Who is Jesus?

He is the one who

Hears my call,

He is my Lord ,

My all in all.

What a friend we have in Jesus,

All our sin and grief to bear,

What a privilege to carry

Everything to God in prayer.

As together we come

As together we've come,

Along the way,

With much to do,

Much to say.

We've laughed,

Maybe even cried,

But as a group,

God for us does provide.

Together through the year

We've travelled far,

Sometimes by video,

Others by car.

We've sat at the table,

And dined,

A time to relax and unwind.

Also, we've had fun,

With quizzes and games,

Though who won,

Well, I'll not name any names.

Most of all,

Together we've prayed,

And learnt more about the Lord,

So let's continue to meet,

With one accord.

Lord bless us we pray,

Keep us safe day by day,

May we be a blessing to all,

And continue to be within Thy call.

As years pass by

As each year passes by,

We all stop and question why

So many had to bear such pain,

Such sorrow

In order

That we could live the morrow

In safety and peace.

May our remembrance never cease,

As each poppy does fall,

May we hear the quiet call,

Always reach out

IN LOVE TO ONE ANOTHER.

Sister, brother,

Let us live in one accord,

As is the will of our Lord.

Tis Christmas time

Tis Christmas time,

Let each heart cheer,

Cast aside all

Doubt and fear.

Tis Christmas time

Let the lights glow bright,

May each heart

Be merry and bright.

Tis Christmas time,

Let the candles burn,

Watch the flame,

Away from all worry, turn.

Tis Christmas time,

Feel the Saviours love

Flowing across the land,

Bringing peace from above.

Tis Christmas time,

God bless you

And fill your hearts

With everlasting joy.

Have a wonderful Christmas.

As you walk along life's way

Tis Christmas time,

Let each heart cheer,

Cast aside all

Doubt and fear.

Tis Christmas time

Let the lights glow bright,

May each heart

Be merry and bright.

Tis Christmas time,

Let the candles burn,

Watch the flame,

Away from all worry, turn.

Tis Christmas time,

Feel the Saviours love

Flowing across the land,

Bringing peace from above.

Tis Christmas time,

God bless you

And fill your hearts

With everlasting joy.

Have a wonderful Christmas.

Hallalujah

Hallelujah

Amidst the highs and lows,

God's love overflows.

Hallelujah

Amidst the anguish and pain,

God's love dost reign.

Hallelujah

Amidst the strain and stress,

Is a God that can bless.

Hallelujah

Amidst all worries and cares,

Is a God who shares.

Hallelujah

In sickness and sorrow,

Is a God we can follow.

Hallelujah

In rejection and despair,

He's with us there.

Hallelujah

Whatever befall,

He's there whenever we call.

HALLELUJAH

THE LORD OUR GOD THE ALMIGHTY REIGNS.

Psalm 23

The Lord is my Guardian

I have many blessings,

He makes me rest in his love

And keeps my spirit calm,

Quenching my soul.

He guides me along the right way

Making sure I stay near to him

Even though

I know my journey will end,

I am not afraid.

For he is always with me,

His grace and mercy.

They give my soul comfort and peace

He pours grace and forgiveness over me,

My soul overflows with blessings

His Love, peace and joy

Are with me always.

When my life's journey ends

I will live in Heaven

With him forever.

Holy Spirit

Holy Spirit

Thou art by my side,

Holy Spirit,

Thou art my guide,

Holy Spirit,

You set my heart aflame

Each time you place upon my lips,

Jesus' name.

Holy Spirit,

Thou dost come from above

In the form of a dove,

Sweeping down to touch my heart.

Holy Spirit,

May I always set apart

Time to seek God's face,

In order that He

Might fill me with His grace.

Holy Spirit,

Your love fills my life,

Within It's joys and strife,

Holy Spirit

As you and I journey on,

You fill my heart

With an everlasting song.

Shades of time

The sleeping creature awakes,

To a new dawn,

The golden daffodils trumpet

Sways in the breeze

On a new morn.

Eastertide comes along,

A reminder

Of why it is

That in our hearts

We can sing a new song.

The golden sun

Shines in a bright blue sky,

Songbirds fly

Way up high,

Flowers with their colours fair

A reminder

That there is joy and hope out there.

Bronze leaves, autumn breeze,

Sights that to the eye doth please,

Animals getting ready

For their rest,

A reminder

How each one is blessed.

Winter approaches like a storm,

Everyone trying to keep warm.

Over the earth doth glow

The purest white snow.

A reminder

That the time has come

For the birth of the one

Who came to save us from above,

Spreading across the world

His love.

Amidst the turmoil and strife

Amidst the turmoil and strife,

Take time to be still

And reflect upon life,

Let the gentle breeze

Blow upon your soul.

Be not afraid,

God is in control.

Amidst upheaval and pain,

Take time to listen

To God again,

Let the cool water

Refresh your soul.

Be not afraid,

God is in control.

Amidst deceit and lies,

Take time to look up

And see the skies.

Give the Holy Spirit

A chance to fill your soul,

Be not afraid

God is in control.

Amidst sadness and joy,

Take time to sit

Focus on God and pray,

Let the warmth of the sun

Burn with desire within your soul,

Be not afraid,

God is in control.

Amidst the problems on earth

Take time for your mind to think

Of the one whose birth,

Brought hope to your soul,

Be not afraid,

God is in control.

Let us join together as one

Let us join together as one,

Now that our praise and worship

Has begun,

May our voices raise

To Heaven above,

Giving God

Our praise.

Holy Spirit come,

Amongst us this day

While we sing,

While we pray.

Joyfully may our hearts sing

Loud Alleluia's to our King.

As together we seek your face,

Fill our hearts with your grace,

Lord hear our cry

As we come before

Your throne on high.

Lift from our hearts

All fear,

As to you

We draw near,

Let each soul be touched with peace,

May our love for you increase.

May we truly be as one,

As we worship your precious son,

Let us join our hearts and sing

Grateful praise to our king.

Come my children

Come my children

Upon this day

Lift up your hearts,

To sing,

To pray,

Let your spirit dance

With joyful steps,

Let your voice

Sing with sweet melodious sound,

May your very being be

Relaxed and free,

For You are in the presence

Of your king,

Therefore from your hearts,

Let loud alleluia's ring.

Come into His presence

Singing Alleluia Alleluia alleluia.

Come into His Presence

Singing Jesus is Lord Jesus is Lord.

Come into His presence

Singing Alleluia Alleluia Alleluia.

Jesus is here

Jesus is here

In this place

Pouring down

Upon us

His grace.

Jesus is here

As together we sing

Our praises

To our Heavenly King.

Jesus is here

As we pray

Giving us strength

Along life's way.

Jesus is here

As the scriptures

We read,

Sewing in each heart

A new seed.

Jesus is here

Whatever we do,

Wherever we go,

Whether we're old

Or new,

Learning what is good,

What is true.

Jesus is here

With us each day,

In our work,

In our play.

May we never fear,

Whoever we are,

Wherever we are,

Whatever we do,

For always

Be assured

That in all

These things

Jesus is here.

Printed in Great Britain
by Amazon